Pocket ACTIVITY FUN and GAMES

DRAGONS

Beware of creatures with glistening scales,
with fire on their breath and poisonous tails.
Many such creatures can be found in this book,
so be brave, open up, and take a look!

This DRAGON book belongs to

....

BARRON'S

What's inside this book?

Stickers

Use your stickers on the dragon sticker scenes, puzzle pages, and anywhere else you want to!

Fun puzzles

Join the dots, find your way through mazes, spot the differences, and play games!

Create and decorate

Look out for the dragon scales for decorating all kinds of things.

Use your imagination

You'll find plenty of pages for artistic knights and maidens.

First edition for North America published in 2013 by Barron's Educational Series, Inc.

Text, design, and illustrations copyright © 2012 Carlton Books Limited

An imprint of the Carlton Publishing Group, 20 Mortimer Street, London, W1T 3JW

All inquiries should be addressed to:
Barron's Educational Series, Inc.
250 Wireless Boulevard
Hauppauge, NY 11788 www.barronseduc.com

ISBN: 978-1-4380-0314-6

Library of Congress Control No: 2012953582

Product conforms to all applicable CPSC and CPSIA 2008 standards.
No lead or phthalate hazard.

Date of Manufacture: February 2013
Manufactured by Leo Marketing, Heshan, China

Printed in China

9 8 7 6 5 4 3 2 1

Author: Andrea Pinnington

A word of WARNING...

Before you undertake the activities in this book, ALWAYS REMEMBER...

- Most dragons are NOT pets.

- DRAGONS do not usually tell the TRUTH.

- If a dragon says he likes you, it means he wants to EAT you.

World of dragons

Complete the dragon pictures.

Mungo, the magnificent

Arthur, the world's oldest dragon

Cecily, the glittering sea serpent

Fiona, the tall and terrified

Sir Robin the Brave on his trusty horse, Kipper

Allegra, the actress

How to draw a dragon

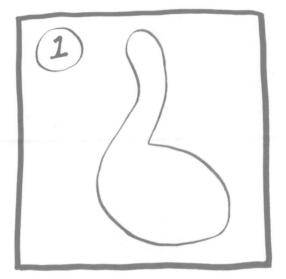

First, draw the dragon's body.
It looks a bit like a thumb.

Good start!

Copy each of the drawing steps into the boxes below.

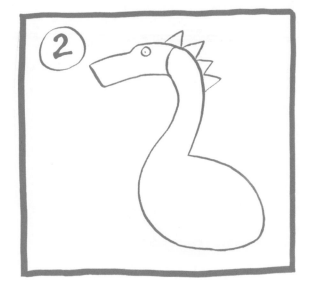

Next, add a long snout, sharp spikes, and a beady eye.

Getting there!

Make it breathe fire and add a
monstrous MOUTH and some FEET.

Almost done!

Finally, give it WINGS on
its back and a terrible tail.

Great work!

Dazzling dragon scales

and what to do with them. . .

1 Cut out the SHAPES on the back of the scaly dragon paper. Stick them where they belong (see pages 20-21) for another dragon job well done!

2 You could use the scaly paper to create a shimmering collage.

3 Cover a notebook with the scales. You can use them for noting down dangerous dragon sightings and details of fearsome fights.

Practice your own dragon scale patterns in the circles below...

Cut these shapes out and find out
where they belong.

Cut out your own shapes here.